Police Officers
at Work

by Karen Latchana Kenney
illustrated by Brian Caleb Dumm

Content Consultant:
Judith Stepan-Norris, PhD
Professor of Sociology, University of California, Irvine

magic
wagon

Meet Your
Community
Workers!

visit us at www.abdopublishing.com

Text by Karen Latchana Kenney
Illustrations by Brian Caleb Dumm
Edited by Patricia Stockland
Interior layout and design by Emily Love
Cover design by Emily Love

Library of Congress Cataloging-in-Publication Data
Kenney, Karen Latchana.
 Police officers at work / by Karen L. Kenney ; illustrated by Brian Caleb Dumm ; content consultant: Judith Stepan-Norris.
     p. cm. — (Meet your community workers)
 Includes index.
 ISBN 978-1-60270-652-1
 1. Police—Juvenile literature. 2. Police patrol—Juvenile literature. I. Title.
 HV7922.K46 2010
 363.2'3—dc22
                             2009002391

Table of Contents

Being a Police Officer

Safety is important! Police officers help keep people safe. They make sure that people follow laws. When a crime happens, the police are called. They go to the crime scene and ask questions. They look for criminals and make arrests.

When a police officer arrests a person, the officer reads that person his rights, handcuffs him, and takes him to jail. At jail, the police officer fills out forms about the person. This is called "booking."

Police officers also patrol streets. They watch traffic to make sure people drive safely. Police officers notice what happens every day in a neighborhood. If something looks different, they check the area closely.

Helping Others

Police officers help everyone in the community. A storeowner calls the police if something is stolen. A lost child asks the police for help. A homeowner calls the police if a robber breaks into his or her home.

Detectives are a type of police officer. They gather facts and clues to help solve crimes.

Police officers try to find stolen things. They return them to the owners. When cars crash, a police officer stops to help. If a traffic light is broken, a police officer directs traffic.

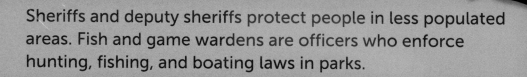

Sheriffs and deputy sheriffs protect people in less populated areas. Fish and game wardens are officers who enforce hunting, fishing, and boating laws in parks.

11

At Work

A police officer wears a uniform to work. It has a name tag and a badge. The officer wears a special hat too.

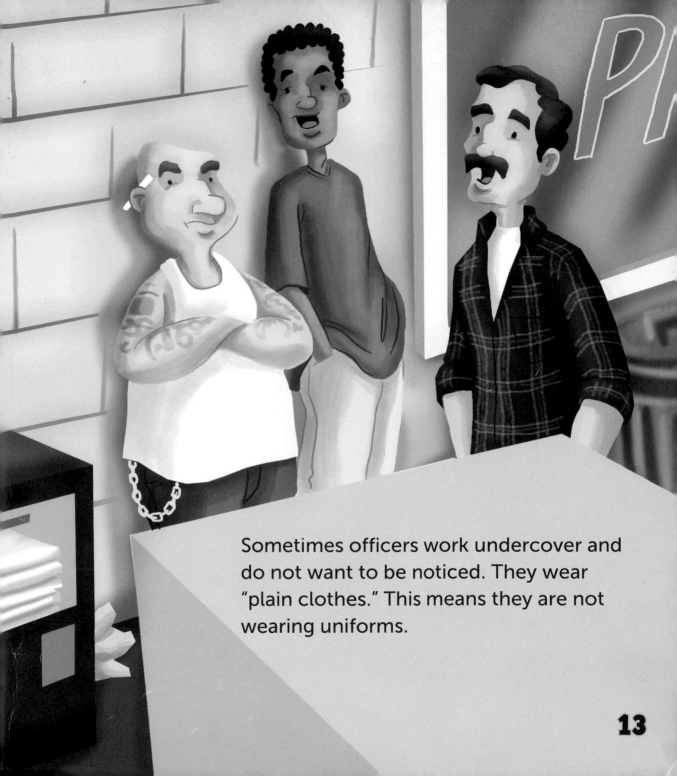

Sometimes officers work undercover and do not want to be noticed. They wear "plain clothes." This means they are not wearing uniforms.

13

STATE PO

Police officers work in neighborhoods and on highways. They are given parts of a city or highway to patrol. They also answer calls from the police department about crimes. Most officers work with a partner. People in the community help officers by telling them facts about crimes.

The area a police officer patrols is called a beat.

Problems on the Job

Working as a police officer can be unsafe. A criminal might shoot at or fight with an officer. Police officers risk their lives for their jobs. It can also be upsetting for officers to see accident victims die.

Sometimes police officers have to testify, or tell what they saw, in court.

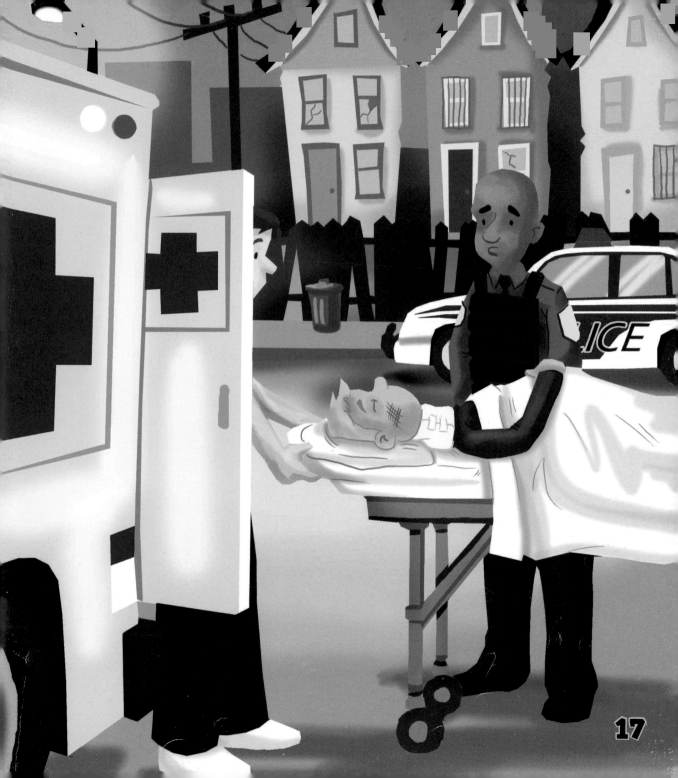

17

Tools Police Officers Need

Police officers use special tools on the job. An officer carries a baton and a flashlight. He or she uses handcuffs when arresting someone. These are put around a person's wrists. If they have to, police officers use their guns. Sometimes officers use dogs. The dogs can smell things officers need to find.

Officers patrol cities in police cars. The cars have loud sirens and flashing lights. Some officers ride bicycles or motorcycles. Sometimes officers even ride horses. Police horses are often used at parades and in parks.

Technology at Work

Video cameras are on the windshields of police cars. They record what happens outside a police car during an officer's day. Mobile Data Terminals are also in police cars. These special computers help officers find the arrest history of a person. Officers use two-way radios to talk with other officers and the police department.

Special Skills and Training

Police officers need good writing skills. They have to write reports about what happens each day. They must think and act quickly when there is a crime. Being healthy and strong helps officers chase criminals and make arrests. Officers need to have good speaking skills. Knowing a second language can also help officers on the job.

Many police officers belong to unions. Unions help workers get fair pay and safer working conditions.

STATE
POLICE

If you want to become a police officer, you need to finish high school. People who want to be officers then train at a special school called a police academy. This training takes 12 to 14 weeks. At the school, students learn first aid and how to use a gun. They also study the law and self-defense.

In the Community

Do you feel safe in your community? Police officers are always working for your safety. They make sure people follow laws, and they stop crimes. Police officers are important workers in every community.

A Day as a Police Officer

Morning

Start the workday at 7:00 AM at the police department.
Leave in a police car to patrol a part of the city.

Late Morning

Stop a driver who is breaking the speed limit.
Write a traffic ticket for that person.
Stop at a business and talk with the owner.
Ask what is going on in the neighborhood.

Afternoon

Answer a call about a traffic accident.
Go to the accident scene and help the injured people.
Call for extra help.
Ask questions about the accident.

Late Afternoon

Drive back to the police department.
Write reports about the day.
Describe the traffic ticket and the accident.
End the workday at 4:00 PM.

Glossary

arrest—an action of a police officer to stop and hold a person who is breaking the law.

baton—a short stick used as a club.

criminal—a person who breaks the law.

police department—the office where police officers in a community work.

risk—to take the chance of death or danger.

self-defense—the act of protecting your body.

stolen—something that has been illegally taken from another person.

union—a group that helps workers gain fair pay and safe working conditions.

victim—someone who is hurt in an accident.

Did You Know?

Sometimes police officers are called "cops" or "coppers." In 1845, police officers did not wear uniforms. They only had badges to show that they were police. The badges were shaped like a star and made from copper metal. People started calling police "coppers" because of these badges.

In the 1800s, only men were police officers. On October 6, 1891, the New York Police Department hired four women. They became the first female officers.

On the Web

To learn more about police officers, visit ABDO Group online at **www.abdopublishing.com**. Web sites about police officers are featured on our Book Links page. These links are routinely monitored and updated to provide the most current information available.

Index

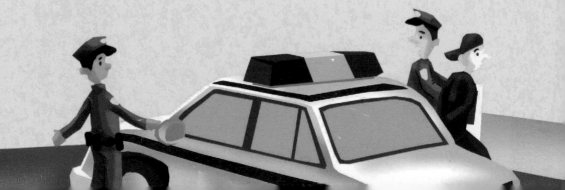